Online Income:

Navigating the Internet Minefield

Ken Courtright

ACKNOWLEDGMENTS

This book could not have happened without the efforts of so many people.

At the top of the list is my wife, Kerri. Kerri has heard me talk about and has seen me physically write books for the past 12 years. The problem is that Kerri also watched me only swing halfway; I wrote the books, but never followed through by actually publishing them. Kerri is the ultimate and forever encourager, not just with me, but with our four beautiful children, Kaci, Kara, Kameron and Kenny Boy. As soon as I mentioned that I was writing a book that was going to come out in late February, instead of rolling her eyes, she said, "I bet it will be awesome!" Thank you, Kerri. I love you more each day.

A pretty close second to my wife and kids are my parents. My mom and dad, Ken and Diane Courtright, as well as my in-laws, Allan and Teryl Lundeen, all played a bit of a role in this book.

From as early as I can remember, my dad was at work at his restaurant. He'd leave around 10 a.m. and come home around 2 a.m., only to do it all over again the next day. I remember when I was seven, my mom told me one day that dad now had Mondays off. I was so excited because I knew I was going to talk him into watching "The Six Million Dollar Man" with me, and I did. After 27 years of long days and nights, and many sacrificial missed events, my dad retired at a young age. Living under that work ethic, and watching that sacrifice of time, did nothing but inspire me to work just as hard. My in-laws, Allan and Teryl, are wired the same way. Although they are supposedly retired, they have multiple rental properties, they are always buying and selling real estate and are currently building their next dream home. I can't thank my parents enough for letting me "watch what they do", instead of "listening to what they say."

Then there is Megan Fitzgerald and Mary Glorfield. These beautiful ladies opened the door to a fantastic platform for the construction and the delivery of this book. In writing the acknowledgements for the book, I noted that while putting the book together, I averaged 11 email and phone correspondences with Megan - PER DAY!

I'd be remiss without thanking the Core of our team at Today's Growth Consultant and Income Store. Mike Engstrom and Todd Krause, long time friends and business partners for years; and Laura Miller, the grease for the wheels in all that we do. I have to thank Mike, Todd, and Laura for putting up with me - as I often go silent for days at a time, not touching phones, email, or any communication platforms.

From a commercial, technical, and managerial standpoint, I need to thank some folks who have mentored me from afar:

First is Brian Tracy. I read Brian's book, "Psychology of Selling" in the mid-nineties and it changed the course of our business. We doubled our previous year's sales five out of the next seven years. After reading the book, our team understood and was able to teach the principles in "Psychology of Selling." Every rep working for us had to understand and acknowledge his or her own individual "income barometer." Understanding, embracing and most importantly, accepting, that single principle resulted in hundreds of thousands of dollars of additional business for us. Thank you, Brian Tracy.

Second is Dave Conklin. Dave Conklin is an internet marketing genius. Dave can be found at www.DaveConklin.org and has ownership in multiple internet marketing companies. Dave helped me understand the fundamentals of how the web works, how search engines respond to site content and site construction, and just how difficult a real internet marketing campaign is to put into place. Dave and I have partnered on many projects throughout the years. Dave has put up with my barrage of calls and texts for the last few years. Thank you, Dave Conklin.

Next is Tony Robbins. In the early nineties I was riding in a car and someone was playing a tape of "Unlimited Power." If I remember correctly, I think I permanently borrowed it. Between "Unlimited Power" and "Awaken the Giant Within" I was unstoppable. Hearing and reading about Neuro-Linguistic Programing (N.L.P) and the story of Andre Agassi's resurrection back to his number one ranking in the world of tennis was not just inspiring it was transformational for me. These books spoke to me as I was not only trying to lead a national team of sales reps, but I was consulting companies that had been around for 50 years. My big challenge was that my sales team's average age was 44, while I was 23; and worse, I had literally no consulting experience when we started. Tony's books and tapes paved the way for me to understand that the limits I have are simply the ones I set for myself. Tony Robbins' mentorship through books, tapes, CDs, and mp3s are a major reason the websites our companies now own will go from 50,000,000 views this year, to well over 100,000,000 views in the next 12 months. Thank you, Tony Robbins.

Finally, I'd like to thank Michael Houlihan and Bonnie Harvey. If you aren't familiar with them, Michael and Bonnie started Barefoot Cellars Wine. They started the Barefoot Wine brand in their laundry room in 1985, made it a nationwide bestseller, and successfully sold the brand to E&J Gallo in 2005. Starting with virtually no money and no wine industry experience, they employed innovative ideas to overcome obstacles and create new markets. Michael and Bonnie are partners of mine on the authority site www.thebrandauthority.net. I was honored when Michael and Bonnie asked me to read the manuscript of their story of how they grew one of the world's largest wine brands with virtually no marketing budget. Their new book, "The Barefoot Spirit", provides every entrepreneur and potential entrepreneur a detailed and strategic look at how to take a company from literally the laundry room of a house, to a global leading brand. It's a remarkable read. The book not only inspired me on many levels, but was the impetus for me to get off my butt and finish something I started 12 years ago, publishing a book. We've also helped Michael and Bonnie share their story with the world with another site, www.barefootwinefounders.com, which provides a more intimate look at Michael and Bonnie, who they are, how they operate and a platform in which to order their book and schedule them for keynote speaking engagements. Thank you, Michael and Bonnie.

Guiding Principle

"If the ladder is not leaning against the right wall,
every step we take
just gets us to the wrong place faster."
— Stephen R. Covey

Here's to those who know that if someone else has done
it, it is just a matter of time...

Contents

PART I

The first five chapters of this book are geared toward two crowds. First, there are those that are currently making money online, but are looking for different approaches or strategies to create more traffic and more revenue. The second is the large segment that have reached a phase in life that has them considering an online income. Both groups have a high likelihood of performing an internet search for phrases like "make money online," "online income," "alternate investment strategies," "work from home," or "money making websites." If you are intrigued by the search results of any of these phrases, then the first 5 chapters are for you.

What's the best way to walk through a minefield? *Follow someone else's footprints.* Those footprints will lead you safely through.

Entrepreneurship and Business Ownership has, for years, been compared to "walking through a minefield." This comparison is founded on the difference between having a job and owning a business. Being a business owner for 20 years, I agree with the analogy. Business Ownership has *hidden* mines all over the place. If we are Business Owners, we can never fully leave the minefield.

When one starts a business, even a small "at-home" business, it is difficult to expect: new competition, changes in the tax code, national recessions and disenchanted partners or employees. We start our businesses in a state of "eternal optimism," soon to realize that it is often better to switch our attitude glasses to "optimistic realism."

When we combine the "Internet" with "Business Ownership," we take the comparison of *"Business Ownership"* to a *"minefield"* to another level. The Internet is filled with even more hidden mines. The landscape that websites play on is forever changing. It is always moving, growing, and adapting. Websites are subject to search engine algorithm changes, new social platform start-ups that *cannot* be ignored and technology advancements that happen at a rate that is hard to comprehend. Website owners are not told of these changes in advance, they simply have to adapt. This highlights that great phrase, "the only constant is change."

Still, with all the variables of the internet, it has never been easier or faster for someone to start a business and generate a tremendous income than it is today.

My hope and prayer is that this book allows you to view our experiences, case studies, metaphors, and "real world" examples as footprints that can act as a path you can follow while navigating an online income. In the ensuing pages, you will see many strategies and examples that were used as we battled our way from zero visits on zero websites in 2009 to over 60,000,000 visits a year across the 200 sites that we now own in 2013.

Filtering Through All The Noise

Have you ever been…

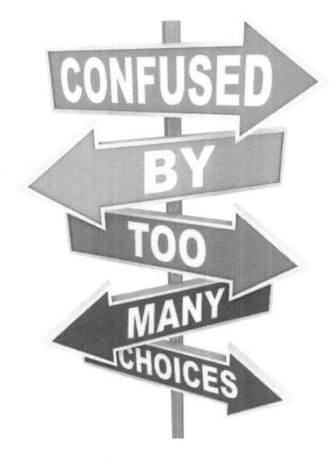

I chose "Filtering Through All The Noise" as the first chapter of this book because of the numerous options presented when people Google something like "make money online" or "how to make money online" or "need extra income."

Over *50* percent of what currently comes up in search, whether it's a paid advertisement or an organic result, features some version of the following:

"Anyone can make money online with our "proven platform". Our platform comes with a website, a landing page, a lead-gen form showcasing our "incredible product". All you will have to do is market it. It is completely turn-key waiting for you to drive traffic to it.

The platform will invariably teach someone how to build a list of interested parties, often referred to as an *opt-in* email list. An opt-in email list is a list of people who have said that it is okay for you email them. They are interested in that niche, or that product, or that industry and they're saying, "It's okay to send me the information that you have."

When the person searching looks at this platform, they often say, "This is great! They have the tool, they have the app and all I have to do is drive traffic to it." They get excited.

When the company says, "all you have to do is market it," that means all a person has to do is build a list of people that are interested in that niche, and send them an offer for the product or service being promoted. If you can build an email list, you will then be able to email them your offer, whether it's monthly, weekly or daily. The entrepreneur will be shown (probably and in most cases) some type of automated software that will send out a series of pre-built email templates that will ask them to purchase the same exact item up to 10 different ways.

Benefits and Risks:

There are definitely benefits and risks with this kind of platform or offering. The unique thing about these platforms is that the benefits and risks are actually the same thing.

The Benefit: This system works. There is no question if you can drop a quality product into a list of people that have opted-in *and* are interested in that niche, *it is going to work.* You will make money.

The Risk: This system works. The first series of emails the entrepreneur sends out are usually well received. The email recipient opens the emails and decides if the product is for them or not. If it is, they often buy it. After purchasing the item, they move on and look forward to the next newsletter or the next "different" product offering you may have. That means that the very next month, you either need to come up with a new product offering to the exact same list or you have to build a completely new list to drop in the exact same product offering. Therefore, this model or platform gets very stale very quickly.

To say it differently, if the platform you adopted sells the newest, latest, greatest model airplane and you spent a full month building an email opt-in list of hundreds of folks that are really into model airplanes than your first email is probably going to sell a good amount of model airplanes. The question is, what do you email them next month? Do you run around and find another product they *might* like that's related to model airplanes? Or, do you build a new list of people – completely different – the very next month and email them the same model airplane offer? Either way, this money-making method is extremely popular: it works very quickly to generate revenue because the offers are usually high quality. The major challenge is that you are left staring at a blank wall in month-two, considering, "Do I find another product to send to the same list or do I build another list for the same product?"

Best advice I can give:

There are three pieces of advice I can offer someone searching for an income online.

The first is to take a similar approach that many take when looking at an income opportunity offline: Evaluate a number of income options before jumping in. The internet offers many great options for creating revenue. Jumping into the first opportunity you explore is literally taking a blind step into a minefield. I suggest making a list of a few questions to consider for your online income opportunity such as:

- How much I would like to earn each month
- How many years has the company been around
- Have I sampled the product
- How much coaching and training is supplied
- Do I have to pay for technical or post sale support

Once you make your list, interview and explore no less than three companies or platforms.

Second: do proper due diligence. You will notice that most online opportunities use some form of "social selling." You'll recognize social selling when you see testimonial after testimonial on their web site. To perform proper due diligence on any online money-making opportunity, the first step is to *email or call the people in the testimonials!*

Although most of the people and the testimonials are real, there is a chance that either their success was fleeting or the claims were stretched. Don't ever take the testimonials and pictures at face value. Unfortunately, it is not that uncommon to have false testimonials, paid endorsements from people who have never used the product, or worst-case scenario, a testimonial that is 100 percent fiction. The people in real testimonials will often respond to the pros and cons of the platform.

When you reach a testimonial contact, or someone the company gives you as a reference, the key question to ask is, "How much money did you make in months three, four, and five?" Ask *this* question, because month one was probably when they did their training, month two was when they most likely spent time building their list, which leaves months three, four, and five to do the actual emailing, which triggers sales, which triggers checks to come in. *Months three, four, and five are when they learn how to build a second list, or find secondary products and choose to either stick with the program or look for a different opportunity.*

Final note on due diligence: if the company doesn't provide any testimonials or references that you can contact, you might not want to add them to your list of money making options.

The third bit of advice is to, *"ride the wave"*. There are a lot of good platforms online that can demonstrate not only how to use the opt-in model, but provide product or service offerings -- pre-built e-commerce platforms or "pay per performance" consulting services. If you find one that provides testimonials and references and are still excited after having used the system and platform for months, if everything else on your list of questions checks out, then jump in and ride the wave of that platform. If an opportunity feels like a good fit, the references check out and it comes with quality coaching and training, it could be the beginning of something great.

DOES EMAIL MARKETING REALLY WORK ANYMORE?

Yes! It absolutely works. However, it is all based on the quality of the email list and the platform being used. The champions of the email delivery industry, such as Constant Contact, have all the "unsubscribe" features, tools and coaching needed to perform a successful email campaign. One just needs to understand that the email delivery platforms can only be used with an opt-in email list. If the email delivery platform discovers you don't have approval for your emails, meaning the list you are using isn't a true opt-in list, they will shut off your service immediately. The platforms will be able to tell that you don't have an opt-in list by the open rate, the volume of unsubscribes and the bounce-backs. Their automatic response is, "Hey, this guy bought this list! The customers did not opt-in."

Further notes on email marketing: Although you can buy a quality opt-in list, it is infinitely better to build one yourself. The best lists are built over time with people truly interested in your product or service. There are a number of people I know that have email lists that could be sold for millions of dollars; they built their lists slowly over 5-10 years. There are also companies that have extremely strong, legitimate lists of leads built around a "double opt-in." A double opt-in means that on a regular basis (from every few weeks, to every one to two years) the leads have to "re-opt-in" to remain on the list. This produces a very strong list of qualified, interested potential customers. A lot of companies make a huge amount of money just promoting new products to an email list they have built over time.

Email marketing absolutely WORKS. It's just a matter of having a proper platform (and knowing how to use the platform) and knowing how to build your email opt-in list.

I'll start a blog and put up "Banner Ads"

One of the oldest ideas online today is to start a blog, generate a following, and then put ads at the top of the page.

This particular idea is "age old." Since the beginning of the internet search bar, bloggers have used websites to display their thoughts and views regarding a certain topic or industry. Blogs allow a person to share whatever they want to say with the world. Blogs are like public journals. Good blogs can pick up large followings. People find someone's blog via an internet search bar or by someone sharing it with them and, one-by-one, the following increases. These large followings can turn into large amounts of income through properly placed ads.

While doing homework to see if a blog is for them, many entrepreneurs find websites showing people making great money from ads. Many people have read the online stories of Markus Frind, who built the dating website "PlentyoFish", and the popular affiliate marketer, Jeremy "ShoeMoney" Schoemaker. Although they didn't use a blog platform, these men display pictures of themselves holding up monthly revenue checks for five and six figures. If you would like a fun exercise, perform an internet image search on "Markus Frind." One of the first image results is of a famous picture of one of his checks from Google for $901,733.44 for a month's worth of traffic.

People see the pictures of these trailblazers' checks and think, "If this guy can work from his mom's basement and make close to one million dollars per month in ad revenue... I could write a blog that could make *at least* $500 - $1,000 each month."

The reality is that the internet ad landscape has changed significantly over the past few years. The amount of money ads pay out "per visitor, per click, or per page view" has decreased quite a bit. These numbers aren't exact, but across our websites we see that the average ads today have settled into a payout of approximately $2 - $10 for every 1,000 hits or page views. That means to make $400 per month from standard ads - you will need to have about 200,000 hits, or "page-views", a month on your website.

When evaluating our sites, we use the formula of 1000 page views equals $2. That means 10,000 views brings us $20, 100,000 views brings us $200, thus 200,000 views brings us $400.

A key factor with blogging is that *every* successful blogger I've spoken to claims that if their blog *never made any money, they would still blog.* They are NOT writing and blogging for the money. The successful bloggers are writing because the information they possess is valuable to an audience. They take great pride in providing that information to their industry or field of interest. They are passionate.

The Benefits and Risks:

The Benefit: Some blogs can absolutely make money. We own a site called www.thisblogrules.com. It's just a blog with basic ads (see the image at the beginning of this chapter). Considering the amount of traffic this site receives, it generates about three times more revenue, per visitor, than the average blog.

Another great blog success story is www.dailycandy.com. This blog started out of New York providing a daily piece of advice on topics such as attire, attitude, where to shop, dining, etc. DailyCandy.com grew quickly early on. It is now one of the biggest sites online today with hundreds of thousands of loyal readers in many cities.

The Risk: To make money from a blog involves much more than just throwing a banner ad across the top of the site. It involves split testing. Split testing is tracking the financial results of different ads in different places on your website. Once you've tried a few different ads in a few different places tracking the revenue, it will be obvious which ad in which position produces the most revenue. Most people don't take the time, have the patience or understand how to perform or read split testing reports. For our blog, www.thisblogrules.com, over 100 ads have been tried and tracked in multiple places inside the site.

Most studies show that over 90% of blogs that display advertising, generate less than $80 per month. They probably gave up on their blog before their audience achieved critical mass, which is a point where a blog is shared virally in an exponential way. Most people start a blog for the wrong reason, which is to *make money*, instead of the passion to contribute.

Best advice I can give:

The only reason to blog is if you are truly passionate about your topic and are convinced that you can add value to an audience. If this is the case, if you blog consistently, you will eventually pick up a loyal following. Part of this loyal following will read *everything* you write. This small group of followers are called "fans" or "ambassadors". These fans are compelled to share and promote the blog. They are your best friends. It only takes a few good fans to create a large following.

Almost all "good" blogs hit a point where the site took off and was able to generate a decent amount of money. I learned from Brian Tracy that this is called "Hockey Stick" income.

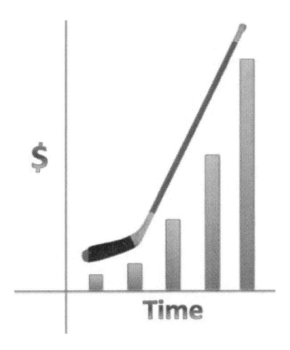

Looking at the above illustration, you will note that the bottom is very short and has only a *slight* angle coming off the ice, but the long handle of the hockey stick comes off the ice at almost 90 degrees.

Financially, most good blogs have gone through this transition. In the beginning, they don't make much money because they only have a small audience sharing the blog with those they know. This area of income is the short part of the hockey stick. If the blogger sticks with it, and stays committed to *"writing for the readers and not the revenue"*, eventually, the audience will grow. With enough fans promoting a blog, it may eventually land in the lap of someone with influence. This person of influence, described as a "sneezer," may share it with their large following. It often only takes one good "mention" by a sneezer and the world now knows the blog exists. With a couple good mentions by sneezers, a blogger may enter into hockey stick income. As Brian Tracy eloquently explains, "Once someone enters Hockey Stick income, they leave earth's gravity and never return."

Most bloggers never experience hockey stick income because they give up on their blog before it hits this inflection point.

In the end, if you are passionate about a topic, confident you can add value to an audience and you would *enjoy* writing a blog – *even if it never made money*, you can't start it soon enough.

WE OFTEN GET ASKED, "WHAT IS SPLIT TESTING"?

The image below is a great representation of split testing. As we go deeper and deeper into a monetization strategy, we keep trying new methods to make money. If an avenue makes money, we keep drilling down by testing and tracking areas within that money-making avenue. If it does not, we try something else.

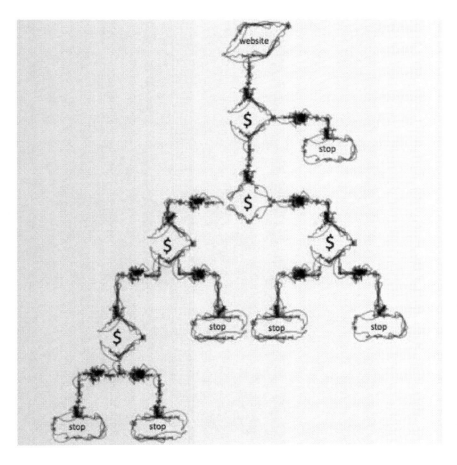

Split testing is often used in two different areas. The first is on the shape and structure of a website. The second is on ad content and placement within the site.

Many website development companies suggest building two websites when building or overhauling a company website. They suggest that you display your company information across two completely different layouts to see which one works better and keeps people on the site longer. This is called "split testing a layout".

In the same way, you can split test a banner ad. Display a banner in the header of your website for a month and track the results of click-thrus. Then move the ad to the footer for a month and track the results of the click-thrus. You may be surprised at the results. This is called "split testing an ad"

A great tool for split testing a layout or ad placement is "Click Tale". Click Tale provides you a tracking-cookie that is placed on your website. The cookie provides information to Click Tale. In a user-friendly dashboard, Click Tale provides a visual view of all the traffic through your site. After a time (a week or a month), you can play a "movie" of all of the traffic on your website. It shows every click that happened on your site during that time. Click Tale gives every click a little yellow dot. When you press play and run the movie, you can see every move the visitor's mouse made by watching the many yellow dots move. These dots show *very clearly* navigation buttons or areas of the site that *never* get touched. If these areas are not being clicked on, you are wasting prime website real estate. You might want to take those buttons or areas down and try something else in in their place. That is split testing.

A Money-Making Website

IS a Business

In the old days, when people came into money, got a great promotion, or even lost their job, you'd often hear, "I'm going to open a restaurant," as if owning a restaurant was an easy way to make money. I can assure you, having four successful restaurants in the family, running a restaurant is *anything but easy*.

In the last ten years, "I'm going to open a restaurant" has been replaced with "I'm going to make money online." It's often said flippantly, as if making money with a website isn't *actually* like owning a real business.

For as many times as I've heard people throw around the phrase, "I'm going to make money online," I've also heard from seasoned business executives and business owners stories of money poured into their websites that are *"still not producing."* As growth consultants, we ask the business owner, "Are you treating your website as a division of your business, or just as a website?" They usually look strangely at us and say, "as a website, of course."

If someone is trying to build a website to produce revenues, the website is a business. This means that fundamental business principles and practices need to be applied to make money.

20

We try to explain to the exasperated business owner that they need to analyze their website the same way they would analyze or evaluate any division inside their company. They need to use the same business reports and measurement methods. Tremendous value is added when a business owner changes their view of a website from a tool or an asset to an actual "business". Only then do they realize they may have been taking their website too lightly.

If you own a website that makes $1 *you are a business owner*. Your site should be treated like a business or at least a division of a larger business. You need to start asking yourself business questions like:

Who are we?

What are we selling?

Why are we selling it?

Who or What is our competition?

What is our competitive advantage?

Why would people choose our site?

What are the two strongest areas of the site?

What are the two weakest areas of the site?

Have we run a S.W.O.T. analysis on the site?

All of the above questions should be asked and answered by anyone that owns a website. You don't have to be an advanced internet marketing strategist, like the guy below, to better understand your website and it's strengths and weaknesses.

The Benefits and Risks:

The Benefit: When you begin treating your website like a real business, you will either save a lot of time and money and not start the website *or* you may learn something you didn't know and build the site or business even faster, potentially making A LOT MORE MONEY. So, before you begin your official journey into "I'm going to make money online," take a day and perform a basic S.W.O.T. analysis on the potential website or online business in question. A S.W.O.T. Analysis (which you can go online and download for free in many different versions from many different sites) lays out the Strengths, Weaknesses, Opportunities and Threats for the site, or online business in question. It can provide great insight into what the business (website) will face once it hits the market and how well it may perform.

The Risks: The risk of treating a website as a business only comes into play if you think that you might fail because you have no previous business experience. I'd hate to think someone didn't start a web-based business because they read this chapter and felt insecure. Most successful website owners have never read a S.W.O.T. analysis or any type of business report. Hopefully, they will read this book and start.

Your online business may turn out better if you enter the arena with no experience reading charts and reports. Number crunching, "report reading"-types don't necessarily make the best website owners. The person that loves a bit of adventure, is willing to stumble a bit and enjoys a challenge is far more prepared to win online.

Best advice I can give:

If you are considering an online business and you have the available funds, locate one of the numerous companies that can run an analysis showing numerical strengths and weaknesses of a potential online idea or concept.

If you are considering an online business and you aren't flush with cash for a S.W.O.T. analysis, but you know in your gut that you will not take the business lightly, *and* you are committed to treat it like a real business (not a pet project), go for it. Start quickly and ask a lot of questions to anyone that will listen.

I'm Looking for Something "Turnkey"

To say that the phrase, "I'm looking for something turnkey" is common, is an understatement. Over 368,000 people typed some form of "turnkey business opportunity" into Google's search bar in December 2012. This means that close to one percent of the U.S. population searched for something that is turnkey. Many people today need extra income. They also probably won't be able to operate a business in their current industry, so they specifically search out businesses that are turnkey.

Ray Kroc, of McDonald's, showed the world that a turnkey operation is a "working model." Kroc's turnkey model is now known as a franchise. It is a model that is tried and true. It is a model that can be replicated to create a fairly accurate *predetermined* financial return. Most importantly, this model can be performed by someone with *no* industry experience.

There are four main components of a turnkey business:

1. The model is up and running. It stands up to any and all forms of due diligence. In short, there is a working, successful model in place.

2. A predetermined return can be extrapolated.

3. No industry experience is required. Anybody can participate if they meet the financial qualifications.

4. There is some form of "out" clause or exit strategy in place.

The Benefits and Risks:

The benefits of a turnkey operation are also the four main components: The model has been fine-tuned and is up and running. It is so fine-tuned that based on either physical location or current website traffic - a predetermined financial return can be extrapolated. No experience is necessary and there is some form of "out" clause where the business owner can get all or most of their money back. Franchise's often come with the ability to allow a franchise owner to sell their franchise, often for a substantial profit.

The only risk is that most good turnkey business models are the franchises available offline (not on the internet). It is also a general rule with a franchise that the less money you invest, the higher the risk of failure. There is typically a direct correlation between initial investment costs and training and advertising budgets. In most cases, the more money invested, the greater the support system and training module. Another word of caution: Franchises are not perfect; they are still susceptible to the landmines of business ownership. Even McDonalds, the most expensive franchise, once in a while has to close a store. Online, the only turnkey model we know of is www.IncomeStore.com.

Best advice I can give:

If "making money" is a deeper need or desire than "making money *online*," then I'd look hard at a good traditional offline franchise. There are some very good franchises with investments as low as $10,000. These franchises come with true gross and net profit models that provide immediate and sustainable cash flow. Because they are a franchise, they come with an abundance of training and support. If you (the franchisee) don't succeed the franchisor doesn't receive royalties from your efforts - which is how franchises generate revenue.

If "Making money *online*" is more important than just "Making Money," due to a lack of any available time, a physical inability to work, a very low risk tolerance, or a need for an "out" or a guarantee of return, the only source that meets *all* the turnkey criteria above, is www.IncomeStore.com.

Understanding Leverage

As in chapter one's, "Filtering Through All The Noise", many people search online for advice on how to make "more money" online. They come across website after website showing people holding up big, fat checks for only two weeks of work. How can that be? The reality is that most of those pictures and testimonials *are* true and are likely the result of using "leverage" over good old-fashioned hard work.

Many people won't consider starting a website because they can't get their head around "market penetration." They wonder, "How am I possibly going to penetrate the market and reach enough people online with my message?" They imagine drowning before jumping in the water.

Just like the root word "lever" describes, online "leverage" involves placing a product or service offering into a large group of people and leveraging the strength and size of the audience. The audience could be Twitter followers, Facebook fans, LinkedIn connections, website traffic or an email list. Any way you look at it, using "leverage" is about getting your product or service offering in front of someone else's audience or sales funnel.

For example, let's say that you just bought the online rights to a product to help people pick stocks with great accuracy. How would you react if your friend called and said that his brother has an investment blog that averages 500,000 visits each month? You would probably drive to your friend's brother's house and *beg* him to do a review of *your* product on *his* website. If you can get your product in front of 500,000 people interested in investing, you just "leveraged" that person's online following. That one product review could make your year.

The Benefits and Risks:

The benefit of using leverage comes when a quality product or service is placed in front of an interested audience. It works almost *every time*.

The risk (or in this case, cost) is that leverage is typically granted quid pro quo. Someone will grant you access to his or her audience or list, but in return, require either a piece of the action or the reciprocity of them gaining access to your following in the near future. You will typically need to offer something in return for accessing another party's list.

Best advice I can give:

First, if you know of a large audience to which you'd like your product or service promoted, start building relationships with decision-makers or anyone on the staff of the company controlling or managing that audience. If you took 2 years to build a relationship with a person or a company that had an online following of 100,000 or more people, how would you feel when you finally get a call saying they will interview you or do a review of your product?

Second, do *not* be afraid to ask. Many times you'll be shocked with the quick response of "Yes." Keep in mind, that the people with the large followings are typically the writer and editor of their own blog. They are often thinking about and seeking out new things to write about. When you come calling and offering them something to review or write about, you are providing them a service.

As a frame of reference: my company has been successful seven times in seven attempts with the U.S. government. After many phone calls and a period of relationship building, we were able to get seven online recommendations from our government (case study explained in chapter 10). By staying professionally persistent, we were able to leverage the audience of some governmental websites.

Shoot for the stars and stay persistent. The dog that barks the loudest gets fed first.

PART II

The following chapters have two goals: Provide insight into the mechanics of Online Income and expose detailed examples and case studies of many money-making websites.

The next five chapters take a close look at everything from "How Google and Search Engines View Your Website" to "making a decision to call in the experts."

Tiger Woods was once asked why he had a coach. A legitimate question considering that at the time he was statistically the best golfer that had ever lived. Tiger's immediate reply was, "That's simple, I can't see my own swing."

The next five chapters allow you to catch a glimpse of the swing of successful websites.

Understanding How Google

Ranks a Website

Nothing would kick-start the second half of this book better than providing a "layman's terms" explanation as to how Google ranks a website. Current and future website rankings should be a part of every website growth strategy. This chapter alone could be a complete book itself.

If you are a "detail" person and would like to see an actual breakdown of all of Google's algorithm (formula Google uses to determine website rankings) changes, there is no better site than Rand Fishkin's www.seomoz.com. On www.seomoz.com, there is a section titled "Google Algorithm Change History" where they break down and analyze every algorithm change released by Google.

For simplicity and brevity, I'm going to provide a 30,000 foot view into "How Google Ranks a Website." Although not literal, the metaphors I provide run close to the real thing.

Few people take the time to understand why their website shows up above or below a competitor. I have seen a website

34

receive *three times more traffic* by moving up two positions on page one of Google's search results page. Here is a CliffsNotes version of how Google determines if a website should show up higher or lower than another site in it's industry:

There are two main factors that determine rankings: "credibility" and "popularity." Let's create an example and take a look at a *fictitious* site called www.abcdoctors.com.

It feels only right to post a disclaimer for the rest of this chapter. Understanding credibility and popularity is <u>mission critical</u> for the success of many websites. Below is a detailed "step by step" view of how Google "crawls" and "ranks" a website. You may want to take this chapter a little slower. Don't feel bad if you start feeling like you are watching Abbot and Costello's "Who's on first?".

Since the mid-90's, a great majority of what Google uses to determine the strength of a website is credibility. The only way for Google to determine a site's credibility is to see what other medical sites think of www.abcdoctors.com. Google simply crawls the website in question to check for other sites linking back to them. Google uses Googlebots, otherwise known as "spiders", to scan billions of pages of content online.

When Googlebots crawl a site, they are looking for many items. One of which is to find, count and source how many other websites have mentioned www.abcdoctors.com. Google can tell if another site has "mentioned" www.abcdoctors.com by crawling www.abcdoctors.com and looking for inbound "links" coming in from other sites. Google follows the inbound links back to the site that has mentioned www.abcdoctors.com. When the spider lands on the mentioning site it reports back to Google's database what site is linking out to www.abcdoctors.com. After a crawl, Google knows exactly how many other sites have mentioned www.abcdoctors.com. To Google the more mentions, or inbound links, the more credible the website. A higher amount of links equals a higher amount of *credibility*.

Let's continue with our fictitious example and say Google crawls www.abcdoctors.com and notices a new inbound link. The spider is built to follow the link. When it does, let's pretend that it ends up following the link to the "tools & resources" section of www.webmd.com. Google is going to say to themselves, "Now wait a minute; we have to take another look at how high we are ranking www.abcdoctors.com since www.webmd.com, *the biggest medical site in our database*, now has it listed as a quality website on its tools and resources page. This mention, or "link", shows Google that www.webmd.com trusts www.abcdoctors.com. In the eyes of Google, that "trust" elevates the "credibility" of www.abcdoctors.com. The graphic below shows how Google sees one site linking to another.

In this graphic, what you see is a picture of www.webmd.com linking to, or mentioning, our small new medical site, www.abcdoctors.com. Google sees this and thinks that this site must be important or www.webmd.com would not have mentioned them.

The key here is that when Google notices the industry leading website, www.webmd.com, mentioning the much smaller www.abcdoctor.com, they immediately change the value that they assign to www.abcdoctor.com. This "value" is known as the website's "page rank". Due to www.abcdoctors.com receiving a new, "higher" page rank, Google then moves it a bit higher in the search engine results pages. Now, due to the higher page rank, www.abcdoctors.com shows up higher in the search results. The image below shows how www.abcdoctors.com moved up in the rankings.

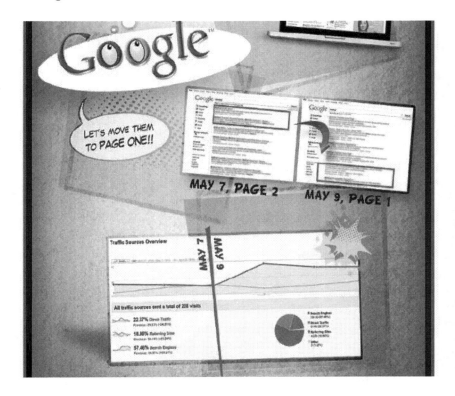

This graphic is a continuation of the first graphic where Google had noticed a link that came in from www.webmd.com to the smaller medical site. On May 7th, Google had assigned a page rank to www.abcdoctors.com on the top of page two for a Google search. Two days later, after Google sourced the link from www.webmd.com to www.abcdoctors.com, they gave www.abcdoctors.com a higher page rank. This new page rank moved www.abcdoctors.com to the bottom of page one in the search results. For years, this ranking system was the dominant way to rank websites.

Google aggressively altered this method throughout last year. Through many algorithm changes, Google shifted a major focus of their rankings from mostly credibility based, which is the *cumulative* value of all the links coming into a website, to a combination of credibility *and* popularity based rankings. For a snapshot of the changes Google rolled out over the last twelve months and a deeper understanding of this chapter check out my article on www.tmcnet.com titled: "The Dust Has Settled Around Search Algorithm Changes.

Measuring rankings by popularity is where we are heading. "Popularity" is exactly what it sounds like. Google measures how many people like the site. Ironically, they don't actually use the site's traffic as a significant factor in measuring this; they measure popularity through "Social Signals". Social signals are best described by imagining that Google has put all websites into a "customer loyalty program". Similar to the points programs offered on credit cards which return "cash-back" based on points accrued, Google has instituted a points program where the more points you accumulate, *the higher your rankings*.

Let's say at 9 a.m. someone shares a piece of your website's content through a Facebook share button on your site. At 10 a.m. someone adds a "Like" to your website's Facebook page. Because of this, you may get a point. At 1 p.m. someone tweets a post off your site with someone re-tweeting the post at 1:10 p.m. The re-tweet may get you a point. Let's say you have a beautiful photo on your site and above all your photos you have "Pinterest share buttons". At 5 p.m. someone "pins" a photo from your site to her Pinterest page; you may have just scored another point. At this pace, by midnight you will have 6 points in Google's new social signal points program. More points equals more *"popularity"*. The more popular, *the higher the rankings*.

There are many other social signals that Google watches for and measures. Suffice it to say, Google watches and measures social signals *very* closely. There is more and more emphasis toward social signals and away from credibility, or the culmination of all your links.

The Benefits and Risks:

The benefit about understanding exactly what "formula" Google is using to evaluate your website is two-fold:

First, if you understand Google's simple over-arching formula of credibility *and* popularity, you can avoid costly mistakes in mis-marketing, or more specifically, "over" marketing your website. Over marketing will be explained in the next chapter.

Second, you can't just focus on credibility or popularity, you have to pay attention to both.

The only risk of gaining a new understanding of "How Google Ranks a Website" would be from inaction. The challenge is that once exposed to this information, you *have to act on it*. If you are like me, exposure to enlightening information can be haunting. It's like the scripture, "knowing the good you ought to do and not doing it, is sin." When I'm introduced to new information that I know will add immediate value, I sometimes can't sleep until adjustments are made.

Best advice I can give:

The best advice I can give regarding the understanding of how search engines operate is to set aside 10 – 20 minutes a week to the continual study of site ranking. The more you understand the search engine's formulas, the better you will *build* your sites and the better you can *market* your sites.

"Internet Marketing Companies"

vs. "Platforms"

Have you had the following experience?

You have a website that ranks for many key phrases and makes "some" money. Still, you are eternally frustrated because you know it could perform much better. To make it worse, you know of others having ugly websites that get much more traffic and make much more money. You've come to the conclusion, "I need help!" You decide, "It's time to bring in the experts." You determine you must hire a consultant or an internet marketing company. Like many, you begin to Google the phrases, "internet marketing companies," "online marketing strategies" or "increase rankings".

There are many outstanding internet marketing companies in business today. There are more great consultants that will work for a fee, or even a slice of revenues. Although we no longer offer individual website consulting, we do support the industry. I hope to clarify, through examples, what criteria to use when seeking outside assistance to aid the growth of your web properties.

A good portion of the search results will not be companies or consultants, but what I describe as marketing "platforms". A platform is a site on which you can pre-select an amount of marketing, or better stated, a number of "links" you are choosing to buy and receive. Once you make a selection, you can go to a shopping cart and buy your marketing or "link" package. You can do this without talking to anyone. These are usually very appetizing options because they are relatively inexpensive for what they appear to offer when measured against the efforts of trying to build a similar link profile in house.

A quick check to determine if you are dealing with an internet marketing company or considering a platform is to call and ask to speak to a rep or sales consultant. You'll know if you are looking at a platform vs. a person or a company if the home page leads with phrases like:

Guaranteed SERP (search engine results page) increase

100 – 500 links

.edu / .gov links

PR 3 to PR 6 links

A price for an amount of links

When this type of info is at the top of the homepage, there's a good chance you are looking at a link-selling platform.

Let's review the last chapter. Google is looking for and more importantly, *measuring* credibility *and* popularity. All of the services delivered by these "platforms" are strictly focused on increasing a site's credibility - and I'm being very *liberal* using the term "credibility." The majority of the link-building efforts these "platforms" offer are far from *credible* links. To make matters worse, the odds that the links being built are within the relevant industry in which the receiving site resides, is pretty slim.

On the flip side, you'll know you have a good chance of talking to a reputable company when you can quickly find the company bragging about it's staff and proudly displaying pictures and bios of the actual folks that will be doing the internet marketing for your site. If you have the budget and you want growth that will be maintained, you have a far greater chance of receiving value from a warm body.

The Benefits and Risks:

The benefit from understanding the difference between companies and "platforms" is measured in the amount of pain and trauma you can avoid by not using "platform" link building services. Google has very little patience for sites that play games and try to game or manipulate their algorithm. To see how serious Google takes this topic, Google phrases like "Google bans" or "Google busts". If you Google these terms, you will quickly see how little patience Google has for companies that try to manipulate search results.

The risk only results if the information is ignored. We have a great internal story of just how serious Google operates when they think that someone just bought a bunch of links:

Years ago, I did a presentation using one of our sites and I couldn't find it anywhere on Google. Turns out, it was banned by Google the day before my meeting.

After a series of emails, we found that Google accused us of "buying" links for our website. In hindsight, if I were Google, I would have thought the same thing.

We spent four months building an "infographic" for one of our sites in the energy industry: (see below)

The graphic has a number of compelling action items regarding energy savings. If every item listed were implemented into the average home, a homeowner could cut their energy bills in half.

We did a lot of marketing and promoting of this infographic. It landed in a Japanese "sneezer's" lap. (sneezers will be explained in chapter 10)

This Japanese blogger, so impressed with our graphic, decided (without our permission) to translate our infographic into Japanese and put it on his blog. 400 of the blogger's loyal followers also grabbed the infographic, shared it, and spread the word. As a result of this marketing push, we were posted on over 400 Japanese websites.

Because the bottom of our info-graphic has a mention and a link back to our energy saving website, those 400 websites provided us with 400 quality, industry related, links back to our energy website. We discovered later that all of this happened in a three-hour period of time.

Google's spiders noticed that 400 inbound links came in to our energy website, *from Japan,* within a three hour period of time. They immediately flagged and de-ranked our website. We were later told that hundreds of links hitting a website in a short period of time, especially from another country, will always raise a red flag. Without coming out and saying it, Google said: "Websites don't receive 400 links in three hours without help." They thought we must have bought 400 links from Japanese websites."

After communicating with Google and showing them our infographic and unauthorized language translation, they looked favorably on us and elevated our rankings. In short, due to our 400 legitimate new mentions, or links, they raised our site's page rank.

The take-away here is that you need to be very careful when attempting to build links. Sacrificing quality for quantity does nothing but cause alarm with search engines.

Best advice I can give:

The best advice is to simply avoid all internet marketing "platforms," PERIOD. But more importantly, I'd like to see everyone "evenly" market their site as opposed to "over" marketing their site ("over" marketing is defined later in the chapter). Since we know a website needs both credibility (links) *and* popularity (social signals), use a rule of thumb that every marketing campaign you roll out alternates between increasing credibility and popularity.

For example, consider next month doing a guest blog post on three other industry sites. This will inevitably provide you three mentions on those sites linking back to your site. In that month, your marketing efforts will go towards link building or "credibility". The smart move would be to make sure that the following month you execute a social media campaign to pick up a few social signals for Google's "popularity" index.

Keep alternating your marketing between credibility and popularity. If you don't alternate, and simply build more links, and build more links, and build more links, you are over emphasizing credibility, or "over" marketing to that element of Google's algorithm. That "over" marketing will get noticed and recorded by

Google's spiders. If you persistently focus on building links, eventually the number of links will be out of the norm when benchmarked against all other sites in your industry. This may raise a red flag with Google, which, I can attest to, is never a good thing.

THE EVOLUTION OF THE WEB

The traffic online in the first decade or so of the web, up until around 2006, was driven on actual websites. This is known as Web 1.0. Web 2.0 was shaped by other alternative forms of websites springing up that work with, support, or even compete with, traditional websites. These alternatives can be used separately or in conjunction with a traditional website (most of them are social alternatives, i.e. Facebook, Pinterest, Twitter, Tumblr, etc). One of the best techniques to grow traffic to your web 1.0 property is to create an under-pinning of your main website with these web 2.0 properties. One marketing technique involves creating a great marriage of eight to fifteen Web 2.0 properties with a main "traditional" website. This marriage makes for a more user-friendly environment for the followers.

We call this marriage "The Walmart approach". Walmart is known as the retail store that offers the most options to purchase. Instead of just one line of lawn mowers, they offer many.

With that in mind, web 2.0 offers website owners the ability to offer a similar approach in acquiring new visitors. Years ago, there were only websites. If you didn't have a computer, or enjoy surfing the web, you never noticed that website, or that business. Today, much website traffic first begins on a phone, a tablet, or even a television. While on any of these devices, you can find a website from a link on a Facebook page, a Pinterest page, a Twitter account and many other platforms.

There is one general rule of thumb when it comes to understanding how many web 2.0 platforms you should manage. "Manage as many web 2.0 platforms as you can manage". Don't start a twitter feed if you don't have time to reply to someone tweeting in. Don't start a Facebook page if you aren't going to update it regularly.

Unrealistic Expectations

We live in a microwave society. There is no doubt about it. We want everything hot, fast, and *now*! When it comes to owning websites, why should our expectations of growth and monetization be any different? I hate to be the bearer of bad news, but when it comes to true, repeatable and predictable online revenues; websites have us sitting in more of a good old-fashioned, slow cooking gas oven.

At TGC and I.S., we partner with investors and industry experts. We build sites that often take 12 – 18 months to construct. One of the toughest obstacles we face lies with our partners wanting revenues to start immediately.

When it comes to consulting work, or partnering on a site, we love setting growth and monetization expectations using the analogy of "baking a cake."

Baking a cake is simple. You use a recipe, which includes specific ingredients, a cooking-time, and baking temperature. We all know what can happen if we start changing the ingredients. Even worse than swapping out certain ingredients is changing the baking time or the baking temperature. Most people know that if a cake calls for 350 degrees and you cook at 220, it will never actually bake; it will come out more like soup - no matter how long you leave it in. Worse yet, if someone sets the oven to 500 degrees instead of 350, that cake is going to come out more like fireplace ash.

That's a great metaphor for a website. Google monitors every website in its database on multiple points. They know how many social mentions and legitimate links the average site generates in any industry. If someone starts a brand new website and immediately buys a link package from a platform, it stands a chance of crashing and burning. Think about it. If 90 days from launch Google notices 1200 links pointing to a brand new site they are going to shake their head and place that site into what is known as the "Google Sandbox". The sandbox is a kind-of a "dummy corner" or "penalty box" where Google sits back for a while and just watches the site. They don't increase the sites rankings even if the site has more links and more social signals pouring in. In essence, that new website owner baked their site at 500 degrees. Talk about stepping on an unseen landmine. Ouch.

There is an outstanding video floating around the web by Will Reynolds. It was a keynote speech at a seminar called MozCon. Will delivers a 30 minute rant about companies getting their heads out of their butts and doing some "real content @#$@#" - we'll call it "real content stuff." Will's rant is about compelling companies to do "real content marketing" instead of buying links.

The key is to set proper expectations on a website's growth. This is determined by the types of actual marketing we do and how long the site typically takes to show results.

The Benefits and Risks:

The benefit of having realistic expectations of a site's growth is that you will be able to more accurately predict traffic and revenues! When you can predict traffic and revenues, you can better budget for more future marketing. It's quite refreshing.

There is no risk associated with having realistic expectations. Realism is always better then fantasy when it comes to business.

Best advice I can give:

The best advice I can give is the old cliché "the truth will set you free." It takes a bit of getting used to, but once you have *realistic* growth expectations for your site, it's quite liberating watching growth and monetization continually go up and to the right when reading your monthly reports.

Website Architecture

Often, after partnering with someone on a new investment website, we get to the part of our agreement where we agree to help them market their existing company website. We have our first strategy meeting and we often hear, "Ken, we've tried everything! We've done SEO, SEM, PPC, retargeting, and media buys. We hired out extra content, we've done infographic pushes and we've spent a ton of money. What else is there?"

One of our first, if not our *very* first question is, "What type of architecture is your site built on?" We usually hear, "I have no idea, HTML?" or, "It's some type of framed site" or, "My cousin did it," but it's usually some version of "I'm not quite sure."

To explain the difference in website architectures we use two examples. First, we take out a piece of paper and draw a large square with a small spider off the top right of the square. We then explain that Google needs to crawl into all websites to see what's inside. Once inside, they will know what page rank to assign that site and where to place that site in their database. Most people nod with understanding.

We then explain that in the early days sites were built, and to a certain degree many still are, with frames. We then draw frames inside the bigger square representing where the logo would go, where the navigation buttons would go, then a frame for where the first content block would go, etc. We basically frame out a drawing of a sample website – and we still have the spider out off to the top right of the drawing. We further explain that search engine spiders can't always get inside the frames. It's up to the website builder to tell the spider what is inside the frames. We tell spiders what is inside the frame by using tags, meta-tags and various types of descriptors. When the spider bumps into the logo frame and reads "abc doctors logo here," the spider now knows that inside the frame is the website's logo.

Here's where things get challenging. Within the content body of the older framed sites, the spiders can't always see into the content block; so they look for the "title section" and other tags and descriptions of what content is in that section. This is a critical issue, because the spiders, most often, either *can't* or simply *don't* read and source the actual content on that page of a framed site. This is why site owners often load up the "buzzwords" or the "key phrases" that are found in that piece of content. They end up "stuffing" those key phrases into the "tag" section in the back end of their site.

Now let's fast forward to today. There are a number of architectural platforms that interact with search engine spiders differently than the older framed sites. There are platforms like Joomla, Drupal, and my favorite, WordPress. These platforms started out as blogging platforms, but have evolved into actual business and commercial platforms as well. Of the 200+ sites we own, 170 are on WordPress. Let's look at why:

First, WordPress is free.

As a simile, these types of platforms are like frameless websites. They are not technically frameless; maybe a better word is slippery. The spiders of search engines can actually read into the navigation buttons, into the content block titles and even into the content of the site itself - even if you choose not to tag your website. Due to the sites construction, in some cases, the spiders can read and source a website down to the last letter of every word on the site. You must put in the same amount of time and care to setting up frameless sites as you would with any other platform, but they are *much more search engine friendly.*

We have a website, www.theplumbinginfo.com, that is about 30 months old. We built it from scratch. We partnered with a plumber in Illinois who wrote a piece of content each week. After 30 months and 115 posts, Google has sent us organic traffic, through their search bar, from over 85,000 different plumbing terms.

Note the graph below. If you look at the bottom right of the graph, it says "shows rows 1-10 of 85,623" terms. This analytics report shows us the 85,000 different plumbing terms that were typed into a Google search bar. The odds of us receiving that type of exposure and traffic from a framed platform - is close to ZERO. If you are doing literally *everything* you are supposed to be doing and not seeing the results you had hoped, especially if your site is quite old, you may want to consider switching platforms.

☐	1.	(not provided)	1.39	00:00:57	92.06%	83.40%
☐	2.	sewer smell in basement	1.22	00:01:02	93.14%	86.88%
☐	3.	theplumbinginfo.com	2.67	00:02:28	15.76%	48.48%
☐	4.	sewage smell in basement	1.19	00:00:50	94.15%	87.10%
☐	5.	freeze proof hose bib	1.42	00:00:49	96.29%	77.07%
☐	6.	frost proof hose bib	1.40	00:00:39	93.37%	78.75%
☐	7.	residential plumbing	3.07	00:02:33	90.58%	45.45%
☐	8.	hose bib	1.32	00:00:43	98.35%	82.64%
☐	9.	plumbing valve types	1.34	00:00:50	95.37%	83.60%
☐	10.	plumbing trap	1.32	00:01:15	86.10%	80.87%

Show rows: 10 ⬍   Go to: 1   1 - 10 of 85623   ‹ ›

Following is another example that helps people understand why their site might not be getting the traffic or making the money they had hoped.

Imagine that you buy tickets to see a famous play and you surprise your family with front row seats. When you arrive you are shocked to see a black ten-foot wall in front of you that *completely* blocks the stage. The curtain lifts up. You can hear the actors come out and begin singing, dancing and performing. Instead of actually seeing the play, the theater provides you with a digital reader board that flashes across a screen showing the CliffsNotes of what they are saying and singing on stage. How frustrated would you be?

That's exactly what you are doing to Google and your audience when you use a framed website. With an old fashioned framed site, you are only showing Google the CliffsNotes of your site, or the "tags." Since they can only see the CliffsNotes, they can only source you for the "CliffsNotes" in their database.

Now let's look at WordPress. It's the same play and it's the same theater, but there is *no wall*. You see the actors and performers. They are right there in front of you, but it's *even better*...there's now an iPad at your seat with hundreds of apps to make the performance even more enjoyable. There are binoculars for those that need them, hearing aids, recording devices, and much more.

When it comes to WordPress, the founder's mindset, when building the platform in 2003, was to create the most user-friendly interface for building and viewing a website. He modeled the architecture after the "app" world. In the app world, our smartphones and tablets have over a million apps to choose from to make our life more enjoyable. We can play games, add a GPS feature to our phones, and chat face-to-face without adding to our bill, all by downloading an app to our phone. Our phones have not changed much in twenty years. We pick up the phone and we dial someone when we would like to talk. Almost all advancements on our phones have come through apps. As life's needs change, so will the apps.

WordPress works the same way. There are now over 1700 WordPress developers that have developed close to 30,000 plug-ins, or apps, for WordPress. As the world around the web changes, like the introduction of Twitter, Instagram, and Pinterest, the world of WordPress changes.

When these new web 2.0 platforms came out, WordPress developers sprung into action and made every possible plug-in so that WordPress sites can move and share content seamlessly into these platforms. Those with sites built in WordPress only have to download the proper plug-in (at no cost) and they are now connecting, communicating with, and probably marketing through, Instagram, Twitter and Pinterest, as soon as they download the plug-in.

WordPress-type platforms let website owners do what they do best, which is promote their message. They don't force website owners to become or hire developers or programmers.

This brings us back to the main point of this chapter. Some have tried literally everything to grow their site correctly. The only thing left to analyze is the possibility that they are running into a wall, or in this case, *a frame*. There comes a time when the "Model T" just has to be traded in.

The Benefits and Risks:

The benefit is to take advantage of the slippery architecture offered by platforms like Joomla or WordPress. Study the top 50 plug-ins that are released every year. See if any new plug-ins make sense for your site and your audience. We send at least one employee to "WordPress Camp" every year to keep up.

The main risk is that if you are on a framed architecture, or an old platform, is that you may be overlooked by Google. Keep in mind, if you decide to move - it can be expensive. Also, WordPress is not the perfect fit for every situation. If you have a large site, an enterprise infrastructure, or have proprietary coding, switching platforms may do more harm than good.

Best advice I can give:

Dig into www.wordpress.org. Talk to at least three people that operate a WordPress, Drupal, or Joomla site and ask them what they like and dislike about the platform. Then ask yourself if it would be worth it long-term to consider switching platforms.

Ken's Top 10 ways to:

"Make Money Online"

The title of this book is "Online Income: Navigating the Internet Minefield". It would not be complete without a chapter providing a "Top 10" list, highlighting some of the best ways to increase traffic and make more money online. Although we've stepped on many landmines testing different site building and marketing techniques, with soon close to 100,000,000 annual views, we've also celebrated the growth of many sites. I've spent most of the book on the underlying theme of "quality" and building things right and methodically; as opposed to over marketing and pushing a site too fast. Being a website owner myself, I wake up every morning and ask myself;

"What's the *fastest* way we can grow this site, or this group of sites, 10, 30, or 100 percent?"

Every site we own has a vested partner who funded the project. For their best interest and ours, it is critical that we are always exploring new ways to grow sites. As I'm sitting in the same "how can we grow this site faster" chair as everyone reading this, I put together a list of my favorite growth techniques. This list is not a "Top 10" list of *theoretical ideas*. This list is taken from the 200 sites we own, marketed, and built, and discerning what tactics seemed to grow the sites the *best* - not necessarily the fastest, but the *best*. The "best" means that the growth was maintained. The following list is in *no particular order*:

* 1 Pure Passion:

As mentioned before, we are partners in a plumbing site. We launched the site and built a "key-word silo." A keyword silo is a list of words and phrases, that if added to a website, will provide Google a better understanding of what the website is all about. After creating a list of 200 keywords for our plumbing partner, I said to myself, "This is going to be one boring website".

I couldn't have been more wrong. The plumber doing the writing, Sean, had 20-years under his belt and was a true expert in his field. He wrote passionately on the key phrases we suggested each week. He immediately began interacting with the people leaving comments on the site - one was the editor of the largest plumbing magazine online. After 30 months, with the pure passion for his topic leading the way, our plumbing partner now sits on the advisory board of a billion dollar company, is nationally known when he walks into a plumbing trade show, and has been filmed on TV multiple times, most recently on the "Giuliana & Bill" show.

Key Growth Model here:

When your site exudes passion for your topic, it's just a matter of time until the site has a loyal following. Nothing beats passionate content. Brian Tracy gave the world a new definition for the word "Sales", stating that "Sales" is a *transference of feelings*. Every website post you write is a sales page. You are selling your readers. You are selling them on you, your opinion and your products or services. Content that is written from the heart has passion. That passion is transferred to the reader. When content leads with passion it has a better chance of going viral, picking up social signals and increasing the rankings of your website.

* 2 User Generated Content:

What if you owned a website that app, tool, and game programmers could use to display their programming skills? What if they actually *needed* your website to enhance their resumes with live samples of their work?

We have one of those. One site makes $500 more each month than the month before and it has for some time. As regular visitors come to the site they see, for example, a new game and they play it. The stream of new games keeps the gamers coming back. We have basic "cpm" banner ads on the site; so we get paid on page-views. It's a perpetual motion machine: the more apps and tools get added, the more people come to the site. The more people that come to our site, the more programmers spread the word that this is the place to show off their programming skills. And the cycle continues.

Key Growth Model here:

Create a platform or carve out a part of your site where you will let people display their work. In exchange, offer them the right to link back to their site. Let them post their contribution to your site on their resume, or claim that they are a "contributing writer" on your website. If you allow others to do a simple "Guest Blog Post", they will share *with their regular audience* that they were mentioned on your site. When they do that, your guest has just exposed your site to their following.

Lets hear it for user-generated content!!!

* 3 Use Leverage:

This is the fastest acting growth model, but it can takes the longest to set up. It's also the easiest to explain. As in our chapter on Leverage, if you can gain access to someone's list, you can hit not only a home run, but a Grand Slam. A home run is when you get a nice burst of traffic for a short period of time because someone exposed your website to their following. A Grand Slam is when the exposure also comes with a strong endorsement. Some endorsements can be so strong and carry enough weight that a good portion of that "burst" of traffic persists as regular followers or fans.

Such is the case with one of our sites. We know someone who knows the actress, Jenny McCarthy. We asked our friend to reach out to Jenny and see if she would check out one of our sites. If she thought it was a quality site, we asked her to tweet about it. She liked it and tweeted. Our site received 100,000 visitors in 90 minutes and we maintained a 2 percent lift, or continued growth, in repeat visitors. Considering that the site already maintained a fairly healthy traffic, that 2 percent was a large sustained traffic increase from a single tweet.

If you have the money, a new marketing method is contracting for celebrity tweets. There are many celebrities that will tweet a message for you. There are laws that state that their messages must come tagged as an endorsement. I've never paid for an endorsement, but based on the results from our celebrity tweet, they may work.

Key Growth Model here:

Find a way to get your website, product, service, or message put in front of someone else's following or audience.

*4 Befriend your top five Sneezers:

Some of you may remember the 1980's commercial that ended, "When E.F. Hutton speaks, people listen."

Every industry has a few people of influence. These are people that may sit on Boards, write nationally syndicated columns, are the editors for large papers or magazines, or just have massive blogs. These people are referred to as "Sneezers". When people sneeze, invisible and sometimes not so invisible, germs spread everywhere. Conceptually, the "germs" are the sneezers' comments, endorsements, and recommendations. Sneezers are like E.F. Hutton, when they speak, people listen.

65

In the marketing world, there are people like Seth Godin and Guy Kawasaki. They spend their lives studying how businesses operate, how audiences respond to a message and the psychology behind why people do what they do. They have enormous followings on their websites and social platforms. *They* are sneezers.

Take a weekend and do nothing but investigate who the top five sneezers are in your industry. The first one or two you will find quite easily because their persona and personal brand is usually front and center in the public eye. The third, fourth and fifth sneezers may take some digging.

Find a way to get to know them. Find out where they speak and attend and shake their hand. That's how I met Brian Tracy, who I consider one of my mentors from afar. He doesn't know it, but his books and tapes shaped how I run my businesses and how I set up my day and operate.

Join their email list, follow them on Twitter, and most importantly, start interacting with them online. Leave well thought out comments on their website that ask great questions that will not only help you, but help any other reader that stumbles on their reply.

It may take three years before you get on the phone or meet them live. So what: they were once where you are now. Most sneezers respect the aspiring person that is professionally persistent; often more than some of the people they work with. Once you get to know them, they can often make a call; suddenly you can find yourself face to face with many, or all, of the four other sneezers on your list.

In the pursuit of a sneezer ask yourself, is there any way I can add value to them? Could you head up a group of fans or followers and proof read the sneezers next book? Could you help moderate a forum? Could you help at one of their conferences? Everyone needs help, including and especially, sneezers.

Here's a great lesson that I love to share: As stated earlier, Tiger Wood's was asked in 2008 why he has a golf coach. In 2008, Tiger was statistically the best golfer that has ever played the game. His response was immediate. "I have a coach, because I can't see my own swing". He asks his coach to review video of his best swing, *hundreds of times*. Tiger knows that if his best swing is ingrained in his coach's mind, *when*, not *if*, Tiger starts digressing from his best swing, the coach can jump in and say, "STOP! Your swing is a bit off." Tiger can then readjust.

I'm not saying call a sneezer and tell them you want to be their coach, I'm just saying that most sneezers know that they have blind spots. Many are very open to true honest offers to help.

Key Growth Model here:

Where Leverage is the fastest acting growth model, befriending sneezers is the slowest. However, once achieved, the sneezer can open doors that no other marketing tactics could ever achieve. If I had to pick one single marketing method to use over all others, **I would choose "Using Leverage."**

* 5 Viral Content:

Make the decision that you are going to write content that has a fighting chance of going viral. Wouldn't it be nice to believe that you *had a chance* of something getting picked up by others and moved all over the web for the world to see? While there is no way of guaranteeing a piece of content will go viral or even predicting if it will, there is at least a way to hedge your bets.

Years ago, we started evaluating all forms of content that went viral. We started writing notes about each piece. Was it funny? Did it have pictures? Did it use charts and graphs? Did it teach? Was it shocking? After a while, a few common traits started appearing. We can say with complete certainty that if you write a piece of content that includes, "The Four C's," you have a slightly better chance of your content going viral.

Take a look at the chart below...

When we collaborate with an author, a business owner or a well-known figure on one of our investment websites, we explain that at least one out of every three pieces of content that we are asking them to write, *has to hit "The Four Cs."*

The Four Cs are:

Cool

Controversial

Cutting Edge

Comedic

If we look back at chapter 7, we discussed the infographic promoted by a Japanese sneezer; it went wildly viral and Google shut us down. That energy infographic showing people how to cut their energy bills in half was Cool, Controversial, and Cutting Edge. Nobody on our staff was surprised it went viral.

We ask our site partners to write content that hits at least one of the "Four Cs" because our analysis shows that a great majority of content that goes viral falls into one of those four categories. We want as much viral content as possible. Viral content builds both credibility and popularity.

Key Growth Model here:

Focusing on the *type* of content you write keeps your web properties fresh and alive. Many site owners get stuck in their own style, which sometimes turns into a rut. Using "The Four Cs" as a guide often energizes the writer. More importantly, the content wakes up the audience, sometimes to the point where they can't help it -- they *have to share a piece of content* with their 500 friends on Facebook; and the content takes flight.

<u>* 6 Try a Content Dump:</u>

Have you ever noticed a correlation between your site's traffic and the overall size of your website? In other words, did you know that a site's revenue potential is often correlated to the amount of content, items, or sections that Google has sourced in their database?

Let's use an example:

If you want to see just how big a site is, open up a Google search bar and type in "site:sitename.com". Don't enter "www.". Just site: then the site name. Let's look again at the internet's biggest medical site, www.webmd.com. Not only is it the largest medical site of all time, it also has the highest medical website revenues, at over five hundred million dollars each year.

See below a chart from MarketWatch.com.

Market Watch — THE WALL STREET JOURNAL.

Annual Financials for WebMD Health Corp.

2007	2008	2009	2010	2011	5-year trend
331.95M	382.78M	438.54M	534.52M	558.78M	

I often wondered how big a site had to be to earn one million dollars. When I found that WebMD.com made 500 times that, I was more than curious of their size. How many pages and sections does WebMD.com have in Google's database? Let's look. In the screenshot below, right below the word "Web" (in red) you see "About 7,220,000 results". That tells us that WebMd.com has over 7 million points of presence in Google's database.

This is great information for someone wanting to create large revenues online. Although large amounts of content is not a *guarantee* of large traffic and revenues, this data gives a web builder a peek into one of the largest sites ever built.

A fun exercise on your own web properties is to calculate the number of content pieces sourced by Google and how much money you are currently earning. Create a spreadsheet and with three columns: Date, Sourced Pages, and Revenue Generated. The chart might look something like this.

Quarter	Sourced Pages	Revenue Generated
1st Qtr. 2012	68	$897.00
2nd Qtr. 2012	85	$1,105.00
3rd Qtr. 2012	88	$1,155.00
4th Qtr. 2012	121	$1,400.00

You will find an interesting correlation between the quantity of content your site has sourced in Google's database and the revenue you generate. Content and sections of your site can also be described as "entry points." If your content and site sections are regularly being sourced by Google, every time you add a piece of content, Google is opening another door to your website to those searching for the information in your new piece of content. The more content, the more doors Google can open. The more doors Google opens, the more traffic you will receive. More traffic equals more earning potential.

I recommend you do a "Content Dump" into a single site for 90 days.

A "Content Dump" pours in as much content as you can write in a 90-day period of time. Before you begin, mark your points of entry in Google's database by running the "site:" report (as we did above with site:webmd.com) on your website. Document it in a spreadsheet with the date. After writing for 90 days, give Google three to six weeks to update their database. Then run the "site:" report on your site again. You have to give Google a few weeks because they crawl sites daily to every few months, depending on your prior levels of activity.

All things being equal, (meaning there wasn't an algorithm change or anything that would skew traffic counts), a content dump will grow the pages and sections sourced by Google. If Google has you sourced in more places, you should see a direct correlation to a bump in traffic on your analytics reports under the section "organic search."

If you aren't currently running analytics tools, I suggest that you run Google Analytics, a free platform, on your site. This traffic tracking software keeps tabs on your traffic at all times.

We see a direct correlation between an increase in traffic with an increase in content. And this translates to an increase in revenue.

Key Growth Model here:

Content gets sourced in Google's database for future search. Consider each piece of content a doorway from Google to your site. More content equals more doors. More doors equal more opportunities to be found. More opportunities to be found equal more opportunities for revenue.

* 7 Quid Pro Quo:

I'll do something for you if you do something for me.

Although I took a hard stance on *buying* links, link *building* still needs to be a major marketing strategy for every site. Search engines still reference how many "quality sites" are linking to your site for their credibility score. We can't ignore link building.

If you are going to take an active role in link building, it is important to understand why people from other websites would desire to mention your website on their website. There are two reasons:

1. Your site adds value to their audience
2. You offer something they need.

Most links are the result of one of these two catalysts.

Let's first focus on offering something that they need.

The links that carry the most weight, according to Google, are links from a governmental website. The government isn't in the habit of throwing out links and mentions. Getting a link directly from a .gov sites is darn near impossible. Google knows this, so when they recognize a link from a .gov website, they increase the page rank of the site receiving the link. As difficult as .gov links are to come by, we've achieved seven links for seven attempts in requesting links from the Government. Here's how we did it:

Years ago, we built a site in the moving and storage business. To compete effectively in this competitive environment we needed Google's attention. We started at the top. We went right for the government. We asked ourselves, "In the world of moving and storage, what role does the government play?" We found that some state .gov websites provide up-to-date lists of reputable movers. These lists help people moving out of state. If you are moving, you can check the government list of registered, certified, and licensed movers.

The government puts quite a bit of work into keeping that list current. We called and asked the following question, "If we built a tool that kept track of all certified and licensed movers in the Midwestern states, will you post our list on your website?" To our surprise and pleasure, the state governments were happy to link to us, as the tool provided an effective back-up when they needed a source to confirm their findings. Once we received a link from the first state, we used this state as a reference. We were honored to have six more states add us to their .gov sites.

Key Growth Model here:

The key growth model here is to determine a strategic value you can add and execute. Some research is always critical to determine the value to the government. We didn't call the government and say, "Hey, it would really help me out if you would mention my site on your site." Instead, we called them and asked, "What could we build that would save you time and / or money.?" Of course, we offered ideas for their consideration.

There is a big difference between asking for a "favor" and "adding value." In essence, it was quid pro quo, "I'll do something for you, if you do something for me."

* 8 Build a simple, but valuable tool:

After studying a very simple and basic site called www.mortgagecalculator.org, we noticed that this simple, two-page website had very heavy traffic and also made a *ton* of money. It was not as much a website, as it is a "tool." This website is more of a widget. It's a calculator that can be ported to any other website.

Real estate agents add this calculator to their website so they can quickly calculate a mortgage with their clients in front of them. Homeowners use it to determine how much they might save if they refinance. It's a very valuable, sharable, and user-friendly tool. Though it has very little content, it has been mentioned, or linked to, by thousands of other websites.

After studying this application, we began programming a "staying out of debt" tool. It's near enough completion to use as an example.

We want to teach people the difference between *spending money* on interest, as in a credit card, student loan, or car payment, and *earning money* with interest, as in a CD or savings acct.

We built a quick calculator that allows the user to adjust a rate they would like to see in a savings account or cd. The beta of this tool is available at http://www.edebtadvice.org/life-calculation/. You can see an image of the calculator below...

AGE	EVENT	ITEM	PRINCIPLE BORROWED	INTEREST RATE	LENGTH OF TERM (YEARS)	TOTAL ANNUAL INTEREST PAID BY ROGER	TOTAL GAINED BY DAVID INVESTING ANNUAL INTEREST PAID BY ROGER
17	Car	Used car	$1,800.00	26%	3	$156.00	$162.24
18					0	$156.00	$330.87
19	Starts college	Student loan	$13,000.00	6.8%	0	$156.00	$506.45
20					0	0	$528.71
21	First new car	New car	$22,000.00	9%	5	$1,080.16	$1,671.14
22	Gets a full time job				0	$1,080.16	$2,861.35

71		0	$1,256.08	$466,281.57
72		0	$1,256.08	$486,239.16
73		0	0	$505,668.73
74		0	0	$525,916.26
75		0	0	$546,952.93

Total Interest Paid by Roger Throughout His Lifetime $122,557.07

Total Interest Earned By David Through Investing Roger's Interest   **$546,952.93**

WHICH IS BETTER?
You decide.

PAID Interest   **EARNED Interest**

Once we built the tool, we converted it into a widget so others sites can grab it and add it to their sites.

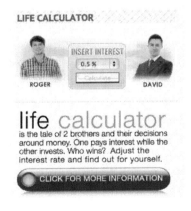

The value of this calculator is simple. By adjusting the rate of savings the brother, "David", will earn, you can see the dramatic difference between living above your means, *spending* interest, and living within your means, *saving and accumulat*ing interest through a savings account.

We believe that parents and teachers will use this to teach the next generation about the difference between interest working *for* us versus interest working *against* us.

Key Growth Model here:

The growth model here is to understand your audience and analyze their needs. If you understand your audience and can anticipate a need, you may be able to create a simple tool or widget that can generate site traffic for years to come.

<u>* 9 Alternate Marketing Methods:</u>

This growth tip or tactic could be a complete book. One of the greatest marketing methods we've found is the shotgun approach. A shotgun, instead of firing bullets, fires shells that explode into tiny fragments. Below is a picture of our approach to marketing.

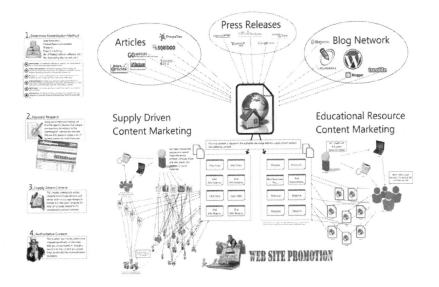

The chart shows that there are many possible marketing options to promote a website. A presence in most major article directories: *good idea.* A press release every month or every quarter: *good idea.* A secondary blog to your site: *good idea.* An app or a tool providing value: *good idea.* A content dump: *good idea.* Do what many successful businesses do and do them all, *track which one works the best*, and then double up on the one that performed the best.

The world changes, the web changes, life changes; is your marketing changing? I suggest that you make a point to try at least two new marketing methods over the next six months.

Key Growth Model here:

Pretend your website is your stomach. Your stomach would get sick of the same food everyday. Why not feed your website something new?

* 10 Get Off-Line:

This may come as a shock, but what may be the single best marketing method used to generate more money *online,* is to go *offline.* Turn off your computer and go meet your industry.

Go to your industry conferences, events and seminars. Get belly-to-belly with the most successful people and companies in your space. Ask a million questions, including, "What is the most successful thing your company is doing online?" Many of the greatest minds in your industry don't put their information online. However, if you turn off your computer, you will find that they are pouring out their wisdom at conferences and events.

I recently learned a valuable lesson. None of my staff could go to the Affiliate Summit in Las Vegas prior to publishing this book. Not really having the time, I made a last minute decision to grab my wife and head to Vegas for a couple days.

I walked into a room of 180 vendor booths and began talking and networking with one great company after another. In the first half hour I was invited to an after-hours masquerade ball at the top of the Paris Hotel.

Sitting in the booth next to me was a consultant that worked on websites on a pay-per-performance basis. He only got paid if he increased a site's revenue. He had a contract with all of the major affiliate platforms.

We worked out a deal to jump into a few of our sites and help us grow them, giving him a percentage of any increase he achieves over our current baseline of revenues. It's a win-win.

Listen close to this next part:

This "website monetization consultant" doesn't have a website! He's a referral-based consultant with a team in the United States and India. He didn't even have a business card! If I hadn't turned off my computer, hadn't stepped out of my comfort zone, and hadn't walked into the room of 180 vendors, I would never have been invited to the Paris Hotel and I wouldn't have met this consultant.

Key Growth Model here:

Turn off your computer, get out of your comfort zone, and get belly-to-belly with your industry.

WRAP UP

I'd be remiss if I didn't wrap up referring back to Chapter 3. Owning a revenue generating website means you are a business owner. If you are a business owner there are business principles that need to be noted. When making money with websites, I often see two traditional business principles abused, or simply ignored. The two principles are;

"The Law of Entropy" and "The Deserve Factor."

Even without specific direction regarding these business principles, if they are put into practice, website owners *will generate more traffic and make more money.*

I've heard these principles described in many ways, but never has there been a stage that *displays their results* better than "money making websites." It is easy to confuse activity with accomplishment and fall into despair, thinking your website has provided all it can.

The "Law of Entropy" states that anything "God Made" or "Man Made" is built to go from order to disorder. In short, everything is built to breakdown and will erode over time. To an exaggerated degree, a car left in a backyard or a field for 80 years won't look anything like it did when it was first parked there. The elements would erode it to a rusty shell with rubber tires. A similar form of erosion happens to all web properties.

With web properties it's happening exponentially faster than the erosion of a car. It is also much easier to see and detect.

The chart below provides an outline of what is going to happen around and to a website.

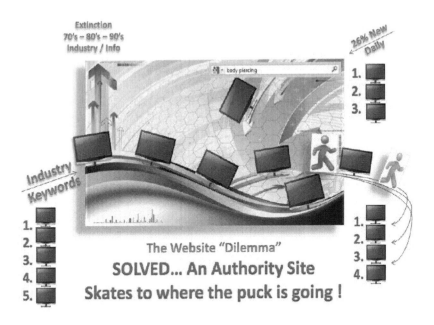

The first thing that happens is the extinction of keywords for which the site currently ranks. This happens for numerous reasons. One reason is the simple loss of interest in the phrases people search for. Do you think people are searching the same phrases today that they searched 10 years ago? Do you think people search online today for the same information that they looked up in Encyclopedias in the 1950s? Of course not. The world changes, information changes, needs change, search phrases change; so should your website.

Between 2008 and 2010, 26 percent of the searches Google received each day WERE FOR THE FIRST TIME!!! That means that one of four searches typed into the Google search bar had *never been typed before*. This one is hard to believe. Today, it's down to about 15 percent, which is still one out of every seven searches. See the chart below.

Google Facts about Google and Competition

| Overview | About Search | About Ads | Better Answers | Transparency |

How Google Search Works

Algorithms Rank Relevant Results Higher

Testing and Evaluation

Manual Control and the

About Search

Every day Google answers more than one billion questions from people around the globe in 181 countries and 146 languages. 15% of the searches we see everyday we've never seen before. Technology makes this possible because

People now type, and even speak, in phrases and acronymns like BFF, LOL, and ROFL. If we are texting and speaking this way, odds are good we are searching similarly. Some of the greatest tools available are Google Trends and Google Alerts. It is often hilarious watching new Alerts come through and new phraseology being used in certain industries. If a site is not updated regularly with fresh, quality, content, the site will not only de-rank in the search engines but it will be obvious that the content is old and stale.

With that in mind, not only do we have to continually keep the key phrases we want to be ranked for fresh and new, we have to keep an eye out for fresh and new platforms as entry points of traffic to our site. Recent platforms include Facebook, Twitter, and Pinterest. To put the importance of this in perspective, our plumbing site receives traffic each month from over 150 different places.

Here's my point: How many sites just five short years ago had regular traffic coming in from Twitter, Facebook, Pinterest, and Stumbleupon? Very, very few - if any. How many sites today get more than half their traffic from these platforms? *Millions.*

If there has been this much change in traffic patterns in a few short years, what platforms will be able to send our sites traffic over the next few years? Who knows?

Here's a great way to look at traffic entry points coming into a website: Imagine that you own a traditional business with a storefront. Someone knocks on your door and says, "Hi, I was just identified as the best sales person in your industry. I don't charge a salary or a commission. Would you like me to come work for you?" If that happened, any business owner in the world would hire that person on the spot.

That happens once or twice a year in the world of the web. Platforms spring up on a regular basis. Once functioning and used, they can send traffic to your site for free. With all these great traffic-generating platforms springing up, many site owners don't know these platforms exist, under-value them, or shrug them off saying, "I don't have time for Twitter or Facebook."

One last analogy of how lightly some take their websites. Let's again use the traditional business owner analogy. This time, the business owner just discovered that the city in which they operate decided to build a new bridge that will re-route 50 per cent of their current storefront traffic. That business owner would, no doubt, pay attention. Their livelihood depends on the traffic driving by their store. Not only would they pay attention, they'd consider moving their location to intersect the new traffic stream.

This is happening all around us and many people owning websites see the "avenues" of traffic shifting. Instead of changing course and embracing the new avenues, they sit back and double up on the same marketing methods they've been using for years. That would be like the retail store owner watching the new bridge open up, see his storefront traffic drop in half, and react by putting up a bigger sign. A bigger sign to half of the people that already know you are there is a waste of a good sign.

As much as I see "The Law of Entropy" ignored by folks just sitting back and doing the same routine, I see "The Deserve Factor" ignored by all but a select few.

The best business analogy for "The Deserve Factor" is a story I watched unfold with the retirement of Michael Jordan. My wife, Kerri, was a Chicago Luv-a-Bull in the mid-nineties. As both a cheerleader for the Chicago Bulls and a brand ambassador for the Bulls organization, Kerri was able to meet Michael and became even more of a fan.

On the day of Michael's final game he was interviewed. Mark Giangreco, the reporter interviewing Michael, got to the stadium four hours early to prepare his notes. To his surprise, Michael was on the court sweating and practicing with a ball-boy continually throwing him basketballs to shoot.

Mark, in complete amazement, walked up to Michael and asked an excellent question.

Mark Giangreco: "Michael, this is your last game, it's the last game of the NBA finals, why would you risk injury and be out here practicing? You can't possibly improve your game and get any better. You are already the best player the game has ever seen."

Michael Jordan: "Mark, I've come out here before every game since I entered the league. I have to practice, "outside of practice," so I can "deserve" to hit the game winning shot".

What is Michael Jordan really saying? He's saying something that can be applied to sports, business, education or any area in which people or companies compete. There is the "Deserve Factor" in play. Other consultants throw around the phrase, "What is your right to win", or, "right to succeed." I think these are similar. If you are reading this book you obviously want your website to succeed. Don't' be afraid to put a little more work than you are used to into your website. The results are worth it.

Since 1992, I've been involved in the growth plan of thousands of businesses and websites. I've worked closely with hundreds of fantastic business owners, executives, athletes, and high achievers. You can almost smell when a person or a company

"Deserves" to win. It's more than just a feeling. These high achievers are compelled to share the new ground they are breaking, the new information they stumbled upon, the new person they met, the book they read or the conference they've attended. These high achievers "practice outside of practice." They go above and beyond for their businesses and websites. They "Deserve" to win.

Wayne Gretzky once said, "I wasn't considered the best hockey player because I was strong or fast. I was considered the greatest hockey player because I always skated to where the puck was *going*, not where the puck was *at*."

High achievers "Deserve" to win. The people that operate the largest money making websites are skating to where the traffic is going. They build sites and monetization methods that are not only working now, but will be working in the future. They are forever in the pursuit of where the web is going, not where the web is at.

These two principles allow you to measure for success. You can use them continually for self-evaluation and the evaluation of your web properties.

Grab a piece of paper and grade yourself on the following:

"Law of Entropy"

In the last six months, I've studied and changed direction on the key phrases I'm adding to my site.

YES / NO

In the last six months, I've studied and added a new entry point of traffic to my site.

YES / NO

"The Deserve Factor"

In the last six months, I've read a book, attended a conference or joined an industry forum regarding my website

YES / NO   (you are reading this book, circle YES)

In the last six months, I've interviewed a consultant, met a sneezer, or did a content dump into my website.

YES / NO

I believe if you scored one YES in each section, you are on your way. If you scored four YESes, nothing can stop you. If you are willing to embrace the principles outlined in this book, it's just a matter of time until your site is one of the top producing sites in your space.

There is a big difference between experience and wisdom. Experience is learning from your own mistakes while wisdom is learning from others experience.

My hope and prayer is that this book allows my online income experiences to act as footprints in this minefield we call the internet.

See you on the trail.

ABOUT THE AUTHOR

Ken Courtright

Ken Courtright resides just south of Chicago with his wife Kerri and his four beautiful children.

He is the founder of Today's Growth Consultant, TGC, and Income Store, I.S. Ken's companies have consulted on over 2000 companies over the last two decades. Both TGC and I.S. partner with businesses and individuals, helping them generate revenue online. TGC and I.S. own and operate over 200 revenue-generating websites with close to 100 industry experts, business owners, industry thought leaders and fund managers. Their portfolio of sites are viewed just under 100,000,000 times each year, with a combined website growth rate of 4,000,000 annual views each month. As one of the fastest growing U.S. companies, TGC filled out paperwork to be considered for the Inc.500 list.

You can find Ken regularly speaking to the entrepreneurship students at Loyola University, helping and contributing to John Maxwell's "Injoy" organization - which focuses on leadership development, or at CTO, helping raise young men lacking a stable home environment.